Benjamin R. Smith a Biography of My Quaker Ancestor

Richard Atwater Lutman

Published by DrafttoDigital, 2023.

While every precaution has been taken in the preparation of this book, the publisher assumes no responsibility for errors or omissions, or for damages resulting from the use of the information contained herein.

BENJAMIN R. SMITH A BIOGRAPHY OF MY QUAKER ANCESTOR

First edition. July 11, 2023.

Written by Richard Atwater Lutman.

TABLE OF CONTENTS

Picture of my parents taken shortly after
their marriage in 1859

PREFACE

FOREWORD

BENJAMIN RAPER SMITH
1825-1904

'Who shall ascend into the hill of the Lord? or who
shall stand in his holy place? H e that hath clean
hands, and a pure heart; who hath lifted
up his soul unto vanity, nor sworn deceitfully. He
shall receive the blessing from the Lord, and
righteousness from the God of his salvation.'

Psalm XXIV: verses 3, 4 and 5
This little account of my father is written for his grand children
ANNA WHARTON WOOD
April, 1943

CHAPTER ONE

Benjamin Raper Smith, eldest of the three children of his parents, Daniel B. and Esther (Morton) Smith, was born in Philadelphia March 31st, 1825, and was the only one who left descendants. Both of his parents came from a long line of Quaker ancestors and transmitted to their little son the finest characteristics of their faith. Like them he was absolutely truthful, with their unswerving devotion to follow The Inward Light as revealed to his own soul. His reverence for the wondrous manifestations of the Creator, around us in every side, also a part of his inheritance, and his keen enjoyment of their beauty, grew ever stronger with his years. You all have access to the accurate and interesting account of the Burlington Smiths, written by Richard

Morris Smith, tracing them back to their paternal ancestor, William Smith of Bramham, in the West Riding of Yorkshire. The emigrating ancestor settled in Burlington, New Jersey, his descendants mostly, remaining there and in the end neighboring state of Pennsylvania.

Esther Morton, Smith's ancestors came from Rhode Island, from the city of Newport, and she was connected with most of the prominent Quaker families of New England, whence she derived an unusual strength and independence of character. Added to these qualities a wide international outlook was hers, which was common to the inhabitants of Newport, in those early days, so important to place the history of our country.

In her book, "The Quaker in the Forum," Amelia M. Gummer gives us a delightful picture of the Newport Quakers. *"The town (Newport) at this period was the metropolis of the country swarming with officers of British Navy, travelers from all parts of the world, mariners who had become prosperous merchants—often in the slave trade, and sometimes by privateering—Huguenot refugees, and representatives of all faiths. The Quakers came inevitably into contact with many varieties and types of thought, and nowhere has it ever been impossible to find a more delightful circle of highly educated and intelligent Quakers than at Newport before the*

Revolution." These words apply to Esther Morton Smith and also to her ancestors.

Owing to the fact that his parents, also were the only ones of their generation to leave descendants, little Ben and his sister and brother had no first cousins, which deprived them of the many joys of childhood. The nearest approach, were several half first cousins, descendants of their grandfather John Morton, by his first wife, with one or two whom my father was intimate with all of his life. However these parents were very devoted to their children, and they were well, if not so somewhat strictly brought up according to modern ideas.

From the time that little Ben was a very small boy, he was taken occasionally to visit his mother's aunt, Abigail Robinson who was the last of the Thomas and Sarah Robinson's children, to live in the old house in Washington Street, in Newport.

The following extract was from a letter written by Esther Morton Smith to her aunt, dated 8. 13. 1826, when her son was about a year and a half old before these visits had begun.

"I hope my dear aunt thee will not love the less my poor boy for having a long chin and upper lip. He is as homely a fellow as need be and is less slightly by far than any

of my grandfather's descendants but in goodness yields to none of the second and third generation. So I hope this will make up for other deficiencies."

(This type of face was very prominent in the family of Daniel B. Smith, and my father, who always wore a full beard, and later life often said that if he shaved it off, no one would know how one would know him.)

This extract, undated, is from Esther Morton Smith, while visiting Burlington, with her little son to her husband.

"Ben is perfectly well and good. Has something pleasant to say to us all. Goes about town making observations, and likes Burlington as well as any Smith of his inches ever did. He certainly is a delightful creature and in my eyes almost handsome tho people will say that he is his father over again—I don't want father to come up here or anybody else. I hate my sister should be overrun with our folks I cannot help hoping to see thee on the 7th day though my note is commenced so philosophically. Do come if thee can."

In-spite of this opinion of his mother, that her son was very young shared the family feeling for Burlington, as she grew older he was not so fond of his visits, though he dutifully went to see his aunt in Burlington, however, he owed his early friendship with Susan Dillwyn Parrish, granddaughter of John and Ann Cox, whose farm Ox Mead was well known and loved, as they were, in the whole neighborhood. One day, when they were both very young, tradition has it, that they were sitting and standing by a fence looking over to the Ox Mead fields, white with the graceful waving blossoms of the wild carrots. Young Benjamin took it upon himself to say that the land was poor where they grew, which was violently taken up by his companion. They both became quite heated about it, and I have heard my aunt refer to the circumstance with much amusement in her later years, still, perhaps having a feeling that her beloved Ox Mead was maligned! The circumstances of their lives drew these two very close to each other as Susanna married Rodman Wharton, eldest brother of Esther Fisher Wharton, Benjamin's wife. Susanna, very early in life was left a widow with two small children, and for many years was a near neighbor of her boy friend Benjamin, who was a tower of strength to them all.

Excerpt of the letter from Esther Morton Smith to Mary R. Morton 8.10. 1828.

"I do think it is rather hard that thee should have been away three weeks and in all that time have written once to me. My dear mother thee forgets that I am, by your leaving us, separated by three-fifths of all I have in the world and I have never before felt so lonely. Yesterday Daniel went to Wilmington and I packed up my baby and took Sarah and him to spend the day with Mary—.It is too dismal there and seems like the 'chamber of the tomb—.'Everything looks so still and fixed—and one's foot echoes almost fearfully. I do not think I shall go again till you come home. She seems well and says she does not feel lonely or timid. I could not live so I am sure—This morning my master was not here to make me go to the Arch Street meeting, so I went to Pine St. just because I was so gloomy and wanted to see some faces that might look kindly at me—, If I were with thee I should have enough to say—but I cannot

when I write think of what I to tell thee or Ashley do pray right to me I dream about you so much and not pleasantly that in spite of the reason I'm often filled with gloomy forebodings about you. Give my love to aunt Abby I hope she will make Ben mind her—and do not dear mother let him disturb or injure the garden. Dear little soul—I long to see him and hear him—. Does not thee think it was strange indifference in me to think of leaving me—could thee—. Think of Bob and then tell me. Farewell my dear mother my boy is calling me for his luncheon fourth time since breakfast and it is now 12 o'clock. He did not wake once last night from the time I went to bed until after 5 this morning and has been asleep two-thirds of the time since. It is delightful to wash him and he enjoys it so much. Friend Morris says he is certainly like father. I am perfectly well have a good appetite and good gruel and good posset every day."

This next is undated, from Esther Barton Smith to her mother at Newport, perhaps on the same is it is the one spoken of above.

"My dear Mother will excuse me for taking up with the fag end of the sheet of paper and allow me to say how acceptable thy letters are to us and how and anxiously we look for them. I fear very much my little boy is greatly in your way and wears out Aunt Abby and patience. Give my love to him, and tell him that he must try to learn from his

*A.B.C's at cousin Sukey's so that he may be able to read
to his father and mother in the Bible about our Heavenly Father. I often think, I cannot hold out for two months
without seeing him. Please remember me affectionately
to Aunt Abby and tell her that if in after years my little
boy shows much of good about him, I shall attribute it to
the joint influence of you two."*

**Mary R. Morton to Esther Morton Smith. New-
port 21st of 8mo. 1828.**

*"My dear Hetty: While I was writing my third letter of
the 15 thy the third of the 10th arrived and was most
welcome to me. I think I told thee that in that same
epistle. Thy complaints the scantiness of my contribu-
tions to the support of our correspondence appear to me
not quite correct: I have written letter for letter since
I left you: and considering that you have two pair of
hands and eyes are favored with pretty good health and
with the exercise of no intellect of no common order, in
full vigor—while I have but one set these indespensibles,
and they, as well as all my other powers and appliances
mental and personal—are sadly on the wane—it seems
to me that I have advanced my full share of the stock,
and that you are pretty largely in arrears. I refer this
case of conscience to your decision and shall go on my
fourth letter as I may! Thou asks me if I do not think
it was very strange indifference in thee to part with thy
son at so early in age, and for such a length of time
and queries if I could have done so. To this to this I*

can truly say and promptly answer to that my own dear mother I have done so.—especially knowing how much pleasure that mother would derive from the loan. His School continues to be agreeable to him as it was at first; he goes very cheerfully every morning about half-past eight, and returns a little after twelve—generally with some highly satisfactory account of his progress in learning, and of cousin Sukie's commendations of him. Today he told me she said she could hardly bear to part with him—and that he had taken a new lesson. He brings his book home with him but is too much engaged in much more active occupations to attend much to it here.I sometimes get him to show me the little 'be c's. I think he knows the names and forms of most, if not all of them and the capitals go to s begins to spell whenever the evening is sufficiently calm he goes into the fish water (duck pond), and is equally delighted with exploits there. He told us last evening that he swam a good way off—the truth of which had to be no doubt. He kneels down in water a little more than a depth of his knees, throws, out his arms, splashes the fluid merrily about, dips in his head, and thinks he swims just like big boys do. Yesterday afternoon Anna Jenkins paid us a visit with her aunt—Ben was clean dressed, talked to the friends, and behaved very handsomely. I think I have not told thee how nicely he is accommodated in my chamber—he has a cot bed between mine and the wall, where he enjoys the sweet and unbroken slumbers usually the portion of youth, health and abundant exercise; and in the morning often into creep into my bed, to take

care of me and tell me his dreams—Twice I have con-
signed him to the Penitentiary, the passage between the
north parlor and the kitchen—once for telling a fib and
persisting in it; and once for perverseness and obstina-
cy. The evening after the first offense when went upstairs
with him at his bedtime I told him it was a good way
for everybody, before we went to sleep to try to recollect
how he had the day and if we and had done anything
naughty to be sorry for it and ask our Heavenly Father if
He would please—He immediately replied, 'I have done
one very naughty thing today, I hope my Heavenly Father will forgive me.' His reviews are sometimes are quite
touching. Last evening he told me he was sure he had
been a good boy all that day—he had behaved handsomely to the friends and had taken a new lesson and
seemed so confident of the care that would be taken of
him, that he declined asking for it as he said he was very
tired and sleepy."

CHAPTER TWO

These happy beginnings of his knowledge of Newport the loved home of his ancestors, grew with the years; they were golden days and when the time came that he inherited it great was his joy Aunt Abby was a strict Friend, a preacher and one of the ways in which she was very particular, was to have rather a long silence before meals. This was hard for a small nephew, hungry to begin again and equally anxious to continue his play. One day at breakfast the steaming fish and the hot Johnny cake were too much for him, his mouth watered so that he could scarcely swallow, and finally he could no longer, and cried out; "fire, fire, fire" in a loud voice. No doubt this was effectual. and that he was punished, as aunt Abbey had decided ideas of the proper disciplining of the young.

The fishermen lived close by, and their sons, were constantly about the water front where there was always something to be done to their boats. They were the native Newporter's, a fine set of men among whom my father made many friends. From them he discovered early in life, the lure the sea, and probably with some help, made this first little boat in which she was allowed to sail as far as the light house on Goat Island. Just when he began to take lessons in a sailing boat, I do not know but have many times heard him tell of going out with John Pike, in one of the small cat boats, developed in Newport or a fishing expedition. On the way home, when sailing before the wind, John usually cleaned the fish, which would be put into the well until the proper time came, and although he was apparently paying no attention to the sailing, he would say, "keep her off for little Benny" or" luff up a bit" which of course was done, These fishermen included the names so familiar to us as the younger generation: Barker, Merritt, Goddard, Pike and Stoddard.

For the first eight years his life, little Ben lived in Philadelphia. When he was three years old, his parents moved from their first home on Arch Street, near seventh, where his father carried on his business, the keeping of a small drug store. In that year, 1828, John Morton died, his widow Mary Robinson Morton, following the next year, 1829, at which time their daughter, Esther Morton Smith with her husband and two little boys moved to the Morton house, 116 S. Front Street. The only other member of the family, then living there, was her brother Dr. Robert Morton. better known to all of us as, "uncle Bob," this brother and sister, the only children of John Morton and his second wife perfectly devoted to each other and it was only natural that Ben should follow in the steps of his mother and consider him all that a man should be, This feeling grew stronger over the years and I think that his uncle had a great deal to do with molding his character perhaps more than any other person.

CHAPTER THREE

In 1833 the family again changed their place of residence, this time to leave the city and go to Haverford, where my grandfather had an important position in the Haverford School, for school for Friends children which was just starting there.

His wife in writing of it says, *"the children are delighted at the thought of going into the country, Ben is to have a horse Johnny, poultry to feed (my father's taste) and Mary a pet lamb."* Doubtless the change from the to the beautiful and healthful surroundings of Haverford, and the greater freedom of the new life was a real advantage to the children, in establishing their health. There was a large and interesting group of Friends in the neighborhood, some of whom were related to Daniel B. Smith, and the atmosphere in which they lived was most congenial.

The following composition written many years after this time by Mary Morton Smith when she was at a boarding school, kept by Yardley Warner, gives us a delightful picture, of which; otherwise, we should know nothing, of the pleasant afternoons and evenings in the children's nursery. The old stove held a very important place in their activities.

February 24-1846

"A short memoir of the Stove which stands in my room.

The subject of the present memoir verifies the old adage that Handsome is that handsome does. For truly would you never imagine at first sight that such a short fat looking stove, could be so useful. And yet I doubt whether you would find one that has done half as much good among a handful of its kind. To look at its face, you would think it had an easy life but, just look close to the pipe and you will be convinced it had done something in its days for there is a large hole which is probably made when, in a great hurry to warm the room. When could this have happened? Perhaps a stormy afternoon when it was almost time for the children to come home from school, being in haste to warm the nursery for them, for you must know it stood in the nursery. How delightful it was. We came home from school in a blustering March day to see it burn so bright and warm with its doors wide open as if to welcome us. I never saw such a place to make molasses candy as it was, and I'm sure I never tasted any half so good. To be sure it was often burnt and we used to burn our fingers too, but you know, those were the days of hope. and we always looked at the end and I assure you, the end soon came to our candy. It had another peculiarity, making a sputtering sort sound of noise which was sure forerunner of a snow storm, it was hailed by us with a general shout of joy. And poor old (mama) had no peace 'till she had mended sleighing caps and mittens and prepared all the mufflers for a sleigh ride Papa was teased 'till he allowed us to take our sleds to be mended and had gone himself to. see if the sleigh wanted repairing.

"But what," said he one day "makes, you think we shall have snow? "Oh," was the reply, "the stove in the nursery was treading snow all day yesterday." If that is the case" said he "there is no use in trying to put you off—so get on our hats and we'll to see to getting things in trim."

I think however the stove was never so bright and agreeable as on the seventh day, night, for it had more to do than any other time. For besides warming the room for fear that the little ones should catch cold, it had the water and the children's clothes to warm after we were all in bed, and mother had come to see if we were all snugly tucked in and had to listen to her sweet voice as she read a chapter from the Bible, then the stove looks so contented, as if it would say "Now they are all safe in bed" I will set the kettle on singing to put them into sleep." And sure went from week to week, through all cold Winter, the same pleasant warm hearted Stove. We were always sorry when it forsook us as the Spring advanced, and delighted, when the cold

November's wind came bring it back to us.

MARY MORTON SMITH

We can almost see the children returning cold and snowy from school or from playing out of doors, their joy over the success of their candy making, although both it and their fingers got burned and hear the (treading of the snow); which was so exciting to them, being the forerunner of another snowstorm.

In my grandfather's book room in our house, in which a coal fire always burned, in winter, was the grate, and I well remember hearing "the treading of the snow," with much interest.

We cannot follow the steps taken by our hero, up the winding road of learning, between cousin Sukey's little school, in Newport and Haverford School. He probably attended the regular schools under the care of the Friends Meetings. But I have recollection of his telling me that, as a small boy he went to the little school gotten up for his own children and a few others, by Henry Cope of Philadelphia, a great friend of Daniel B. Smith. The teacher was Bronson Alcott, and the members of the Cope family, whom I asked could tell nothing of it. But a biography of

Bronson Alcott (F.B Sanborn and William T. Harris) shows that for a short time he was in Pennsylvania, and was invited, under "auspicious, conditions, to open a school among the Quakers of Philadelphia and Germantown." This was done in 1831.

Bronson Alcott enjoyed his intercourse with the Quakers, and mentions especially, Ruben Haines, his near neighbor, whose son married a daughter of Henry Cope. The school flourished for a while and then dwindled. In 1833 it seems to have ended, on a second school was opened in Philadelphia with fifteen pupils. Little Ben was then eight years old, so this is probably the one of which he spoke. It was also very short lived, and Bronson Alcott returned to New England.

To the Senior Class the Professor of English Literature (Daniel B. Smith) gave a large share of his time and care. Dugold Stewart's Philosophy was carefully read aloud to them by him, and in such an intelligent manner that it could not fail to interest; while this extraordinary course of ethical elections left on their minds impressions of truth which can never be effaced. To them, under the Divine blessing, more than one of his pupils owed their clearest perceptions of the great doctrine of Christ as a Deliverer and Savior. (Haverford College 1830 to1890).

CHAPTER FOUR

It was my father's great desire to be a physician, largely, perhaps as his Uncle Bob belonged to that profession, and if he had been allowed to follow in his steps, he would have been an outstanding one, having in himself the necessary qualifications i n a remarkable degree. He was strong, both mentally and physically, clear-headed, sympathetic, and understanding, and in an emergency could always be depended upon. The circumstances of his life, however, made this impossible, although there were many occasions upon which he was called to help out in nursing, there being at that time practically trained nurses.

In 1852 when he was twenty-seven years old, Lindley Fisher, was one of the old Haverford School students, died in Germantown of smallpox, which several of his friends helped in taking him out of there. He died in one of the small houses in old Wakefield, where he was taken to be separated from his family, and my father was with him during the last night of his life. Instead of studying medicine my father went to the drug business of his father, the firm being Smith & Hodgson, the latter being an English chemist of good standing. He was a very plain Friend and was quite upset by a theater which was directly opposite to their shop; when the crowd was going out or in, my father told me with great amusement how "Billy" Hodgson would elbow among them. right toward them remarking at intervals in a loud voice;—"den of inequity—sink of vice!"

After this my grandfather formed the partnership consisting of himself, his son and Henry

Pemberton a bright and capable young chemist, under the name of Smith, Pemberton & Company, which did not continue for many years, and was his last business venture. The business failed under circumstances which were considered dishonorable by the Meeting, and father and son were disowned.

The former was re-instated sometime later, at his request, but his son was never again a member, which in his later years would have been a great comfort as he was a strong Friend.

This   whole circumstance and what it involved in a changed feeling towards her husband, in many cases, was particularly hard for my grandmother, who, I think never entirely emerged from the shadow of the cloud. After the firm of Smith and Pemberton & Company went out of business, my father was for some years a drug broker, with what success I do not know. Although it will interfere somewhat with the sequence of the story, I shall now tell of his last business venture. His father's good friend Mr. Pow-ers, of the firm, Powers & Weightman, known over the country as being one of the best chemical plants, asked my father to go in-to business with his son-in-law, Jay Campbell Harris in the man-ufacturing of plaster. Mr. Harris was in the Navy when he was married, which is one too many for Mr. Powers who thought of this way out. It did not long continue however, partly because Mr. Harris wanted to be the boss and re-sented the position given to "old Smith." Although the firm was doing good work it suddenly came to an end one day. A long paper was drawn up and to be signed by my father which when shown to Mr. Powers, was immediately torn up, and another submit-ted saying: "I hereby release Benjamin R. Smith from all financial obligations."

How pleasantly this fit into the family plans will be told later.

Sometime after when Mr. Powers died, and my father was asked to be one of the pallbearers, and received, with the others, a large and handsome piece of black velvet, I think to go around their hats. which made a stylish "waist" as it was then called for by my mother.

CHAPTER FIVE

In 1836 the first break occurred in a small family circle, in the death of the second son, John Morton Smith, whom my grandmother did not hesitate to say he was her favorite child. He died of a contagious disease, I think scarlet fever, and what would today could be called the criminal disregard of the laws of health, the other children were allowed to play, as usual in the room which the little body was laid. Her idea perhaps was to teach them, beginning in the early years, that death was not to be thought of with a terror and aversion, and was but the natural end of life's as birth was of the covenant shrimp. This lesson played an important part in my father's life. In 1849 my grandfather moved to Germantown, where the remainder of his life was passed. At that time it was quite removed from Philadelphia, and had a distinct character of its own, largely given by the Pennsylvania Dutch for whom it was named. The Main Street, which connected the nearby country with Philadelphia, was a great thoroughfare for the farmers who brought their produce of different kinds to the city, especially just before market day. Their large covered wagons were a common sight and with themselves in their simple country clothes, not unlike of Quakers, made a pleasant picture. Many of them had regular customers, and would stop weekly, leaving poultry, lamb, chickens, eggs, and butter. This custom still persists, my brother's family getting these things from descendants of the man who served his grandmother.

Some of the beautiful houses built by the early inhabitants are still standing, giving us an idea of the prosperity, comfort and thrift of their owners. One of the best preserved was built by David Deshler and is known as "Washington's Headquarters," as he made it his home during his stay in Germantown. I always feel that we are connected with the house, as David's daughter, Esther, the first wife of John Morton, for whom the precious only daughter of the second was named. When this daughter was seriously considering matrimony, it was some time before she consented to marry Daniel B. Smith, but about the time that she had made-up her mind, she was heard to say, with great decision, that "she would you rather marry Daniel Smith and live in a pill box, than Samuel B Morris, you live in his grand house." I always supposed that the remark applied to this house but it was not bought by him until 1833, it does not fit the story.

The Germantown houses were built on the road, in every sense the center of town, and, and like the old English Lanes, considerably below the level of the sides, necessitating, often, a short flight of steps to reach the front doors. Beside the large houses there were many smaller ones built of the gray stone, so common in the neighborhood; over the tops of the front doors "pent houses," on either side which were placed benches, on which the habitants sat, in the cool of the evening, to gossip with their friends. For the town was a sociable place.

A fine example of this latter type is the one still standing on Main Street, at the corner of east Johnston, known as the Billmeyer house it was a double house, having two front doors and little stoops, and in it my father and mother began their housekeeping.

In Germantown, as at Haverford, there was an unusually interesting and cultivated group of Friends, with whom Daniel B. Smith had been connected from his early days, notably Henry Cope and Lloyd Mifflin. The house chosen by my grandfather was an unusual and attractive one, partly covered with ivy, at the corner of Main Street and Walnut Lane, which separated it from "Wyck," the ancestral home of the Haines family. The families of the two friends corresponded in age and there was the greatest intimacy between them,

These early years in Germantown, were the happiest in the lives of my grandparents. Mary Morton Smith was then an early womanhood, an unusually bright, pleasant and amusing girl, much loved by her friends and the center of the group, two of them naming their first daughters for her. Her face bore the marked characteristics of the Smith family, as described by her mother Aunt Abby. She was of a very affectionate nature, devoted to her parents and to her brother, although I hardly remember to have heard my father speak of her, and it was through Francis Cope I heard of her charming personality. Her particular friends were the families of Rueben Haynes and Henry Cope, Jane Morris and her brother Wister of Overbrook; the Wister girls and Susan Israel, of the Waln family. Two young men, Thomas Stewardson, a Smith cousin, and Edward Crenshaw, a promising young chemist from Richmond, Virginia, were members of the group. These young people were privileged to share the simple and delightful hospitality offered by my grandparents, and none of them ever forgot cousin Hetty Smith's influence.

In 1854 my aunt died and the following extract from a letter of her mother's gives an idea of what it meant to the family circle.

"I believe there was no happier family than ours.—It seems as if the thing least expected has come and I am no more the same.—When Ben comes home in the evening I am always cheerful—and if company comes—I do not wish to force my griefs upon anyone. I have had a full share of happiness I know, and know too that I could not ask for my sweet daughter half that she is now in possession of—Our house is almost left unto us descolate—poor Ben has lost and dearest friend—indeed I think his loss is greater than ours. Her last care, the very evening she died was for him. She asked the girl who stayed with her during tea time what she had made for Ben's supper and charged her to remember him always and see that he had something good when he came home in the evening. She told Hetty Thomas who was her most kind and gentle nurse to instruct Ben how to prepare food for the night—told me how the delightful it would be to have been near her all night—closed her eyes in sleep and waked in Heaven. No one has a more amiable and affectionate child than I have in my son—and since his sister has left us, his gentleness has redoubled. But these troubles have banished them from society and I dread him sinking into indifference to the world. He is in good business now and I hope will pay his debts someday."

This extract shows that my father spent her last night with his sister.

My father, as with probably the case with many of his young Friends, wore a plain coat, about which the Quakers were then very particular, the principal difference being, I think, in the collar, which was much like that of a priest. he was occasionally taken to the Theater by his uncle Bob when so could when made the change I cannot say, but I've heard on reliable authority that he was afterwards handsome was rather distinguished in appearance. He was very popular in this set among them who were the Wister family with its large connections.

He took a number of little trips with parties of young people, one being to Niagara Falls, and used to tell us with amusement that one of the girls insisted on keeping her money in her stocking which arrangement was both complicated and inconvenient. As was to be expected he had several affairs of the heart, but perhaps they only served to strengthen his devotion, which finally settled call my mother, the daughter of his own mother's friend and cousin, Deborah Fisher Wharton. These two had much in common in their heritage, their mothers Mary Robinson and Hannah Rodman having left their Newport homes, in the same year 1793, both to marry Philadelphia Friends much older than themselves. They lived on Front Street almost next door to each other, on the river which was then the nicest part of the city, and their children were very intimate. Indeed I've heard my grandmother Wharton say that when her dear Esther Morton was sent to Westown Boarding School and she could not go, it was a bitter disappointment for her. When the separation came, the family of John Morton were among the very strong Orthodox Friends, and that of Samuel R. Fisher, equally so on the other side. This naturally made some difference in their intimacy, and I've heard my father tell, with amusement, his meeting "Friend Fisher" one day on the street, whose question: whose question: "Well my little man, what is thee going to be on the grows up, the reply was given with much to "I'm going to be an Orthodox Elder."

I think it was in a small party at aunt Barker's house (my father called her husband "Abe" and knew him well) that he first met my mother when she and her sister, aunt Annie were enough to be of interest to this rather particular cousin who had seen something of the world. He must have known Annie before, as he gave her a flower, during the evening, thereby causing the younger sister a pang of jealousy. It did not take my father long to make up his mind as to his wishes, and the two young people saw a good deal of each other.

The following is an extract from a letter written by aunt Annie, 5th mo. 8th '58, when she was paying a gay visit to aunt Haydock, in New York where the younger sisters generally went together.

> *"My dear Het, I do wish thee was here today only selfishly I own, for thy letters show a good deal of enjoyment, but then here it is perfectly splendid, there never was anything more charming. I only want thee, everybody does everything for my pleasure and I have had enough attention. I warrant thee to offset thine—. I am really concerned for Benjy, it looks remarkably like real to me, take care Pinky don't go too far, a little is fun but is much is dangerous."*

This letter shows that things are well advanced in a little over a year my parents were married.

Some members of my mother's family were not very enthusiastic, one of his sisters remarking: "that as you did hope Hetty was not going to have her head turned by a few wildflowers." My father, loved these as few people do, and it was one of the most valuable lessons he taught my mother, to see and enjoy the beauties in the so-called common things around us. There was a corner of the garden at Bellevue, the beautiful country place had been given to William Morton by his father Charles Wharton and was the summer home of the family, my mother particularly loved. vegetables and some small fruits grew in the garden, as well as flowers and it boarded and lovely wood lot.

Here the important words were spoken, one magic afternoon, with no thought of refusal on the Ladys' part. When my father told his mother she replied: "Ben Smith," which she often called him, "I am happier than I thought I should ever be again."

CHAPTER SIX

I wish it were possible to put into words the feeling that my father had for the so-called weaker sex. It combined the chivalry and romance of the knights of old, for their own chosen ladies for whom nothing was too good, with the reverent urge, what he never forgot to do everything in his power to give them the opportunity to fulfill their highest destiny.

The way in which he invariably treated my mother was so marked that one of her sisters in laws, who would have very much like the same, once said; oh, "Oh, Ben Smith treats Hetty like the Queen of Sheba!"

In thirty-four years I was privileged to live with them, in the little differences that must come up, I can truly say that never remember a cross word between them, and my father never tolerated the slightest criticism of my mother from any of his children.

On account of the different points of view of the two families, it was somewhat complicated to arrange for the wedding, which however, came off very successfully at Bellevue, on the afternoon of June 8. 1859. The place which was beautifully planted and laid out, was at its best, the garden was full of flowers and all of the strawberries needed grew in their own vines, and were picked that morning. My mother has told me that she remembered very well seeing her mother, sitting at a certain table every morning, where the fresh fruit was brought in for inspection. Much of it, she prepared herself. This however, does not apply to the wedding day. It was a time of great feeling for my grandmother and aunt Annie, these three having almost inseparable since the death of my grandmother, but they forgot themselves and happiness of the bride. The only outward mark of feeling came from "the little parlor" where Mary Haydock and Sue Wharton, with their small children and rather emotional, lifted their voices aloud and refused to be comforted. When asked what was the matter they said they were crying "because Aunt Hetty was getting married." The two bridesmaids were aunt Annie and Sally, then a girl of fourteen, who was almost like a younger sister to these two aunts. Robert Wln Ryers, intimate friend of my father, waited upon Annie and Horton Baker, just cousin Sally's age was her groom's man It was a great occasion for the two children, and my mother has told me of the care and pride. with which your little niece tried on her wedding slippers, putting a piece of paper on the floor, lest it be dusty.

The bride and groom spent that night at Bellevue and started off the next day on short waiting trip which included Niagara Falls, then very popular when our family went there in 1893, my father looked up their names in the Hotel book; "Ben R. Smith and wife," which we young ones, thought rather a queer way of putting it.

It was not really a part of the wedding trip, but in that fall, my father took his wife for her first visit to Newport which was a great event, not only for themselves, but for four old people living in the Robinson house, who knew this young cousin from boyhood, and loved him well.

Among my sister's papers we found that account of the visit, written for us by my mother, which rounds out our picture, and shows how soon she fell under the spell of this old home which was to mean so much to her also.

"My dear children: In October, 1859, I first went to Newport with your father and his mother. The sail along the sound while daylight lasted was very beautiful; night came on but enough were in no way dampened the enjoyment of my party, who in nearing Newport were approaching the spot on earth dearest to them. I was yet to learn its spell, and arriving there about 2 a.m. saw nothing to interest or cheer. We walked up for the Long Wharf to 33 Washington Street over I rough pavements and sometimes in the

middle of the road and I remember how ma said she almost stumbled in the darkness over some projecting step or stone: "I feel as if I knew every one of them." Little did I know then how she felt, now in 1874, I can much better understand. When morning broke the day after we arrived as I looked out on the dingy houses around us, all unpainted, to my eyes they were the picture of desolation and discomfort while inside inmates and house seemed to belong to a past generation which I had not before known, and while all was kindness seemed little to me to enjoy. Gradually however, I became used to all these and liked to hear ma talk to her old cousins Mary and Amy of times and persons gone while the beautiful day at the west was slowly stealing its way into my heart. It was there always, always unlike one day what it was the day before, and always inviting us to sail. I had never but once or twice been in a sailboat, so that the pleasure. He gave us was as new as it was delightful. Proving a pretty good sailor we went out often and sometimes for a day, while I was learning to know what Horse Head Beaver Tail and what point Judith meant. Another point in my education was advancing as the fisherman one after another man met "Benny" and came to see his wife. Imagine my surprise as a stout old fellow talking to me by the hand said:—"Oh yes Benny's my boy," and then after having been presented, "well Hitty do come and see miss Mrs. Pike." This of course, was John Pike to whose early training in sailing and boating your father does the indeed know his knowledge if not some of his fondness for the life upon the water. He says that many a day he has met the man at the earliest dawn of a summer morning to go with him far out on the day to draw his lobster pots. They would have a soggy time getting out, it would be intensely warm, and the boy would feel sick, but he was learning manliness and endurance, and enjoyed it so much they never failed to go again on the next opportunity offered. A walk to the south shore of the island, some four or five miles, did not daunt us then, and on bright sunshiny days, cloudy damp ones we went tither and we're who are we set by the hour watching the waves dash over the rocks. Sentiment sometimes forsook in favor of reality and turned our thoughts from the beauty of the place to the mushrooms we could gather. Thus looking, listening, sailing and walking about a month passed, when we took up our abode again in Germantown I found Newport had many charms. The two following summers we stayed at home and when we next saw Rhode Island, we took our two little boys with us. It was the east parlor that Bill first for two or three words together and burst out: "dear itty kitty," in admiration of a cat he saw there, to our great surprise and delight. After this we went each year and each year learned to love it better, until in July 1874 we took possession formerly of the old house which had belonged to your father's great grandparents. That year we arrived about 9 p.m. and after taking up a cup of tea and hasty survey of the house we tucked away the children and then lay down to rest ourselves. How can I tell our feelings now as we tried to sleep in the old mansion which had sheltered four generations before ours and seemed almost peopled with their spirits. We wished they might be able to tell some of their experience, for with revolutionary times the old house is associated and much of interest is no doubt hushed in the graves of those now gone—".

My mother has told me what a unique household it was, and that she hardly knew, at first, how to take them. Especially Job Wilbur, who was a real pal, always called Joby, me Ladawax.

CHAPTER SEVEN

Although it is perhaps not particularly appropriate to include in this account, I shall trace the relationship to Mary Williams, which I looked up last summer. "Quaker Tom" Robinson's sister Mary, b.1736; d. 1776. Mary 1757 John Dockray of Newport, son of Benjamin Dockray, of Wigston Cumberland, England. Their daughter Mary Dockray married in 1790 David Williams, of Newport, a famous clockmaker, whose reputation went beyond his native city. One of his clocks is, I believe, it is in the Newport Historical Society, they had three children; Mary

Williams, well known for many years as keeper of the boarding house on Washington Street,

Amy married John Wilbur, an apprentice of her father in the clock making business, and the son David Williams, whose wife was Hannah Brown of Providence The latter became a very dear friend of my mother in the years that she would take us young children, to spend short time in Newport. We always stayed in the house, which is now St. John's Rectorory, which was cousin Hannah's special part of the establishment. Cousin Mary I do not remember but believe that she and her cousin Amy, who is difficult and unassuming, were rather unexpressive, as is the New England way, but cousin Han-nah was one of the friendliest and loveliest of the old time aristocratic Quakers. She lived in Philadelphia after 1874, with her son Dr. Horace Williams in a small house on Pine St., and how she did miss Rhode Island, especially the Point; she said she thought the moon did not shine at all in Philadelphia, being accustomed to its beautiful reflection on Narragansett Bay. After this long digression, I will say that our grandmother and cousin Mary Williams were second cousins!

During her first visit to Newport, my mother, of course, met the Robinson cousins who were then living there and also the Hazard family, with whom my father was so intimate. They lived in a house on Kay Street for many years, two unmarried brothers and three maiden sisters one of whom, cousin Anna, and my parents both considered the pattern of what a lady should be in breeding courtship and hospitality. Cousin Joe who built at Narragansett Pier, many years later, the Hazard Tower, a well-known landmark, was a great walker and with him my father tramped over a large part of the island one of the joys which he never forgot.

Before this Newport visit, my parents were set in the Billmeyer house, before mentioned which although small and unpretending, had both charm and distinction. Many of the family heirlooms, prized by his parents, were joyfully given to their son, among other things, a large part of the now priceless China, brought my Captain Drinker on his ships when he sailed The Seven Seas. It was a common saying that "Ben Smith and his wife have the handsomest China of any of the young couple in Germantown."

The neighborhood was a choice one. Directly opposite, in a delightful little house lived Edmund Crenshaw, with his wife Mary and their two small children; the mothers sat in the windows on the street and the children went and came with great freedom. They were also near to the old Johnson house, Cliveden the fine and aristocratic home of the Chew family, then occupied by Miss Anne Sophia Penn Chew, I think the last of her generation, whom I remember being taken to see is a small child. She was a very warm friend of my grandmother's and living with her two nephews, Sam and Ben Chew, about the age of my father, whom I knew well. About this time that he was married, Sam also took unto himself a wife, Mary Brown, daughter of David S. brown, a prominent Friend of Philadelphia, whose children were near our ages. When my sister Hat and I were old enough to go to school, we were asked to join a little class, very special, that was you gotten up for Anne and Bessie Chew, but it was thought better than we should go to the friends school, the beginning of the Friends School that you know and love so well.

Not very far from the Billmeyer house lived William Dorsey, whose second wife was uncle Haydock's sister, and I wish that you could have gone into his quaint and attractive little China store, the like of which is unknown in these days. It was presided over by a woman to match, and almost any kind of China could be bought, including funny little toys. Cousin Lizzie Dorssey was a great friend of my mother's, and after she was married, of my father's, whom she always called "Neighbor Smith." Opposite the Dorsey house was the very nice, old one of cousin Janette Johnson, mother I think, of the unfortunate Sarah, who sometimes felt called upon to speak in our Meeting, though of the other branch, invariably told to sit down, which she did in tears greatly to the interest of us children. Then came my grandfather's house and Wyck, and a little further down, Vernon, the home of John Wister, where lived Miss Anne who had a tame eagle. My parents lived in this house for about four years, and here their two little boys were born Robert Morton named for his uncle Bob and William Wharton, for his mother's father. There was not quite a year between them, which probably caused the rather delicate health of the latter, worrying his parents, at times, very much. They were fine little boys. It was a great change for my mother to leave Bellevue and spend the summers in this little house, but I truly believe she never once thought of it because of the richer happiness now hers.

CHAPTER EIGHT

I love to think of the pleasure and satisfaction that my grand-mother Smith had with her two little grandsons, who were near enough for her to see every day and brought back some of the joy that had gone from her life. In 1863, as there was another baby coming, the Billmeyer house was too small and the family moved down to Cottage Row, which you will remember. The chosen house was the first in the row, built for Charles Willing, on the Thompson estate, he having married one of the daughters. It had a good-sized lot back of it, facing the Thompson garden, and practically joined that of John Jay Smith, so that it seemed quite country like.

In November 1863 my aunt Annie, who had been in failing health for several years, died of tuberculosis, an unspeakable sorrow not only to her family but to a large circle of friends. She was a woman of unusual strength and independence of character, combined with great charm and sweetness. My mother never entirely recovered from her loss, although it was a slight comfort to have a little daughter, who at least had her name, born in the following January. The only thing that I remember to have heard about my birth, is, that the nurse who had been waiting in house for several days, picked out the night before my appearance to fall down the back stairs, which was not a particular help. My grandmother Smith, though she loved her little boys dearly, said 'that the little girl went straight to her heart," she having lost her precious only daughter, and took greatest pleasure in holding me. Even such a tiny person stirred the chivalrous feelings of my father, who told my mother I must have a new little carriage, the one used by the boys not being good enough; so he had some kind of wicker one, especially made.

Perhaps a year or more before this, my father joined the Home Guards, of which a company was formed in Germantown, containing many of his friends, among them the Wister boys. They drilled in a large market house nearly opposite to ours.

The following letter was written by my aunt Annie, who was staying with my mother, to their mother, and seems of special interest to us today. It is undated but grandmother has written the date 1862.

> *"My dear mother: Please come over to see Het, she is so distressed about Ben's going although she says very little about it. All Germantown will be in mourning today for all the young men are off. Dr. Wister, Wm. Furness, Rod Wister, Ellicott Fisher and plenty of others as well to go with Ben so although we feel most for Hetty there others to pity as well-We shall probably have better news today, the swelling of the streams by the storm yesterday is mostly in our favor, the rebels cannot advance or retreat, and if our leaders know what they are about no traitor will set foot upon the soil of this state. Fan goes to town this morning to hear about her brother, she fears he went with the 15,000 last night—think of Phila, sending so many on only 12 hours notice—5000 more to go today. Please bring your bonnets over. Thine lovingly.(signed) Annie."*

The reason for the special call for troops, the only one to which my father responded, was that the southern army almost in Pennsylvania, which, however, they only touched, owing to their defeat at Gettysburg. The Germantown Home guards, did not arrive until the battle was mostly over, and being tired by their march, they were allowed to lie down for a little rest. It was very short, as the order soon came; "Tumble up boys! tumble up pack your knapsacks and fall in!" which I have heard my father say for the benefit of small children. There was no fighting for them, although they did go onto the battlefield after it was over, and my father picked up some buttons, from both sides, which he brought home in a small tin box, where they still are. The company was mustered out in ten days or so and great was the rejoicing when the men came home without injury. My two grandmothers felt very differently about their sons taking part in the war; my father's mother said she was only sorry she had not twenty sons to send while grandmother Wharton felt it would almost have killed her if one of her four had gone. As a child I remember feeling somewhat ashamed of the latter position, but now I'm much more in sympathy with the C.O.'s.

There was one other time when my father thought he was going to have a peep at the southern army. His parents, about the beginning of the war, went to visit a friend of theirs living in Virginia and everything was so uncertain and unsettled that my father felt best satisfied to go down and wait upon them back. One hot summer afternoon he was going along a quiet country road. when he distinctly heard the sounds of horses' feet coming towards him and wondered if he might be near to the soldiers. In a short time, a cloud of dust arose and he was beginning to think he must be right, from out of it came a southern lady on, horseback followed by a colored man with a large parasol or umbrella where she was holding over her.

CHAPTER NINE

In October 1864 little Bob died of scarlet fever, and my mother grieved over him exceedingly. She rarely spoke of him, but for many years her face was very sad.

This mention of my father and his two little sons, is from a letter written to grandmother Smith after little Bob's death, and adds another touch to the picture of old Germantown which I have tried to give.

"It is a very short time since I stopped twice in a walk, one afternoon, to look at thy two sons as they were walking with their father making such a happy group. I thought how pleasant it was to see a man giving so much attention to his little boys—how much better it was than to be all day long trying to heap up money for them, and how he might hoped to be repaid by their affection, and full development of their noblest facilities. And so, I trust, he, and all of you will be, and even more now are. The dear boy so lovely and interesting in his early bloom is not lost to you, even while you are here—"

The letter was written by Mary D. Haines, wife of John.

In the following February my grandmother, Esther Morgan Smith died of pneumonia, only two months before a little namesake came for her also, bringing her own sweet consolation. You can see from this narrative that in the first years of their married life my parents had only great joys but great sorrows, all of which were keenly felt by them both. Without my father's faith and loving consideration, which made him a variable tower of strength, it would have been impossible for my mother to carry on as she did.

Although my father had had no experience with children he was from the beginning very understanding and unusually fond of his own, who in their part loved him devotedly.

One of my earliest recollections is of the Sunday morning breakfasts which he and I used to have, when he was not so hurried as on the other days. My little chair would be put close to his. So that he could oversee the eating of my bread and molasses, in itself a real treat. We also had long talks about the condition of his factory, which was always in need of cleaning, and nothing would do so well as "Mrs. Doten," his pet name for me, to bring over her broom and

sweep it out.

He was naturally especially devoted to little Het, his mother's namesake a very sensitive and beautiful child, with blue eyes, his favorites, golden hair and an unusually white skin, which at the slightest provocation became a delicate pink. She was rather slow and often late for breakfast, to make up for which she sometimes slighted the necessary preparations, so that my father would say to her before kissing her; "Brushed her teeth? Washed your face and hands?" he once wrote her a little verse.

Only learn to hurry, Het,
Tender hearted, loving Het
I think she'll beat them all Anna, Bill, and Dempsey yet.

When we were children our parents had a number of delightful Christmas parties for the family, including all ages, looked forward to and enjoyed by everyone. The preparations were very simple compared with the elaborate ones of today, but there always a tree, with a small present for each, and sometimes verses would be written.

I remember that Lizzie Wharton wrote one once be-ginning:

Our family, one family,
Are gathered once again,

At the home of dear aunt Hetty And genial uncle Ben.

Uncle Ben was a great favorite, specially perhaps, with his older nieces. He was quite ingenious and once got a little doll, a man, which stood in a corner, and when a string was pulled, raised his hand and threw a sugar plum. The children loved it, but little Hetty who would not go near it and said: "I do not like that little man!" which disappeared which disappointed her father.

On July 5th, 1868, was born the third and last little daughter, Deborah Fisher Smith, named for her maternal grandmother. This fine child—strong, healthy and of unusual promise— lived only eight years, and died I suppose of appendicitis, not then un-derstood. She died in Newport and greatly did we miss her lovely, bright spirit.

About 1873, another crisis arose in a large family, the illness of Hetty Wharton Thurston, n amesake a nd l oved n iece o f my mother, who had tuberculosis of which both her parents died. She was advised to go South for through the winter, but there was no one to accompany her until my mother agreed to do it, taking her four children and a nursemaid. My father could not leave his business, so uncle Bill lent a man in his office, who took us down. We three little girls were dressed alike in navy blue suits, each wearing over her shoulder a small leather bag given by our grandfather with our initials thereon. Traveling in those days was very different, no dining cars, and uncertain stops, so my mother carried a large lunch basket containing a chicken, bread and a can of instantaneous chocolate, a great luxury. We went by boat to Norfolk Virginia, and then by rail, our first stopping being Green Cove Springs, on the St. John's River, where cousin Saunders Coates, his wife and brother had been going for some years. We spent a few weeks there, and then went on to Enterprise, a little further south.

CHAPTER TEN

Once on the trip, when my mother was very lonely and low in her mind, she was asked by a perfect stranger if Mr. Hulse, our conductor, was your husband, replied with greatest feeling; "No unfortunately, he is not my husband." which was capable of two interpretations.

At Enterprise, I think, our party was made complete by my father, whose business had come to an end, as previously stated, and who added much to the pleasure of us all. The place was more in the country surrounded by scrub pines, frequented by many pigs, big and little, with its own pier for the convenience of the river boats, and when my sister and I visited it some fifty years later, looked about the same. The pier was made of wood, running some feet into the river, with a track on which a small car delivered the baggage to and from the Hotel. The incline to the river made the speed quite exciting to us. We spent a good deal of time in this way until my mother was told that it was very dangerous. The river was full of alligators, some large ones, which we used to see sunning themselves on the banks, and one day a man from the Hotel went out rowing never to return. It was supposed that he went swimming was eaten by one of them, which of course, made a great impression on us. In the woods not far away, was a sulfur spring, where any of the guests who wanted to do so could take a bath in a small wooden house, just big enough to hold a top. It was quite popular, not with us, until one day a moccasin snake was found there, which being deadly, put a stop to that pleasure.

One day little Debsey, who had of course heard of all of this, ran to our parents' in great excitement, crying, "father and mother, I have seen a live moccasins snake!"

There are many wild orange trees in various places, having beautiful large fruit, but it was so bitter that we could not use it. My father, who had never been to the south, enjoyed it very much and we took many pleasant walks with him. In some places we saw a great deal of fragrant and beautiful jessamine, and in South Carolina made the acquaintance of the fortune's yellow rose, which I have never seen later.

From Enterprise we went to St. Augustine, a delightful place, then still baring marks of the old Spanish days, including the gate of the wall which surrounded the city. We stayed at a small house kept by a southern woman, who made no pretense of hiding her feelings towards all the hated Yankees. The house had no plumbing and in order to reach the outhouse one had to cross a small courtyard over which a large and fierce drake was lord. Whether he had been instructed by his mistress is unknown but as soon as any of us appeared, he flew at us with loud squawks and bit legs in earnest.

At Saint Augustine we had a little sailing and a favorite place to go was Anastasia Island, not far from the coast, where was a wonderful beach with much coquina. This interested us greatly, as it was compound of millions of little shells, welded together into solid rock, by time and the forces of nature. On the way north we stopped for some weeks in Aiken, South Carolina, which suited cousin Hetty as the climate was lovely and she made some friends of her own age.

But the trip had no material effect and in the fall of 1875, she died at her house in Germantown.

When my father's business ended, my parents went very carefully over the financial situation and decided that by practicing economy they could just break even. What this meant to my mother and to us children, words cannot tell, for it was now my father's greatest desire to do all in his power for us in his delightful way. Nothing was too much trouble and he often interrupted the even tenor of his ways by doing, with us, things which he would not at all have chosen for his own pleasure; notably going with us little girls to Thorps dam on a cold winters afternoon. Unlike his friend Samuel Mason, then quite an old man, still a fine skater he never went on the ice, but waited patiently until we were ready to go home. We have learned many things since then, of which at that time we knew nothing.

CHAPTER ELEVEN

My father had a good baritone voice and if he had taken a few lessons would have given much pleasure to his family and friends. When his two small boys were sick he would walk about, carrying them in the evening, and singing a song they liked very much. He loved the English Ballads, no matter how sad they were, but more than the Scot songs of which I never tired. Occasionally he would sing one himself, with much spirit, but he was always extremely modest as to his accomplishments. As my sister grew she was very fond of singing which was an important part of her simple little parties, many of our friends having a good voices, inspite of the fact that they took any lessons, guitar or banjo, as it was at first, was the accomplishment and she herself always knew the words so we were not restricted to one verse which is often the case. Father never tired of hearing her.

The year 1874 was a memorable year indeed, for us all, as it marked a great change in our lives, bringing us untold happiness and health. For it was at that time that our father and inherited the Robinson house in Newport. Of course it was to us from the first, as it had been to him and his forbearers, the dearest place on earth. No changes were made in the house for the first year, but in the second my father engaged Charles F. McKim, who with much interest, made it as you know it today. He was just starting on a his very successful career as an architect, and although he, perhaps, would not have done it in later years all that he did, it was very satisfactory.

There were now five children in the family, as the youngest, a precocious little boy, who was born on January 18, 1875, and given the name of Edward Wanton, a common ancestor of my parents, for whose memory they had the greatest veneration. My mother's mother was from this time until her death, a member of the family in summer, and she too, loved Newport dearly as being the home of her mother Hannah Rodman Fisher.

My father's joy and pleasure and all of this was unbounded and he at once began to make plans that his sons might know and love the water and boots, as much as he himself did. His fondest hopes were realized.

It is a great pleasure to recall the ways in which our father taught us to love nature, in its various manifestations, of which he was one of the most reverent and appreciative of students.

Every Sunday afternoon no matter how hot, he would walk with us through the fields of the Dyer farm, then quite wild, extending to "Taminy Hill," a corruption of the old Indian name Miantonmi, where we found a variety of beautiful flowers.

My mother, thus speaks of her walks in the paper, quoted before.

"The walks on First day afternoons must not be omitted as they cannot be forgotten. Those you took year after year with your father and all through the summer our rooms have been adorned with the beautiful wildflowers which you carried home; first the delicate Iris, then the lovely wild rose and fragrant honeysuckle, later the magnificent swamp lily, the superb cardinal and aster, and lastly up to the middle of October, the exquisite French gentian. You know what long trips you took for them and how jubilant you were, returning with hands and

*arms filled with your treasures and the pleasure you had
had—Edward always jumped over the fence at the corner and was the first to lay his flowers on my lap, a com-
pliment always grateful and highly appreciated.—"*

When my father really became a part of Newport, in this
way, his enthusiasm and interest in connecting the past with the
present were delightful to see. Many of the family connections,
with whom he kept in touch, we're still living there, and among
the fishermen he found the familiar names and some of the men
whom he had known, grown old like himself. Among these old
"Nels" Merritt was the prime favorite so I have three word pic-
tures of him, my mother's Esters and my own.

Several times in the course of the day we see this picturesque
(figure) pass our house, never varying more from a sober quiet
man than enough to give a slight nod of his head or make some
remark about the weather. He is a handsome man with Gray hair
and beard, a dress which always looks just like the same age and
his head down as if in deep thought. The truth perhaps maybe
perhaps may be not that his thoughts are so deep but his life
of exposure and hardship, has thrown a somber hue over everything. One day when some mischievous boy had cut a hole in our
new fence your father found old nails filling it up with potty and
we were quite proud to be numbered among his friends.

"Almost, before him I should have mentioned 'Dummy
Comstock,' who also wanders up and down our street daily a
mute but keen observer of wind and weather and most things
that take place in his site. Your father learned when a boy to talk
with him by his hands and one day he came into our house where
they had a long talk by the chimney corner. With quite a grace

he enquired some of the particulars of our family, whether I was the wife, how many children we had etc., and his parting blessing when we came away in the autumn was really touching. He is an old man with good features which have learned to express much without words, and his raised eyes with hands folded as if in prayer make a vivid picture of the blessing he asked upon us. His quiet race will soon be running fair and we shall miss him—". I never remember to have seen Danny Comstock but have heard my father speak of him out often and believe, that in his day, he was a fine builder of the Newport cat boats."

The two following extracts are taken from a diary, kept by Het in 1885, when she, Edward and I had gone on to the Newport before our parents brought on our great grandmother and her retinue for the summer.

"Old Nels Merrick still walks up and down the street, but not so often as he used to, and seems to be a good deal older. I thought I noticed that he had on a new pair of trousers the other day, but such an astonishing fact ought not to be credited until positively ascertained."

"Poor John Barker has had a very hard time this winter. One of his daughters was sick and he had no way of paying her doctor's bills except by selling his boat, which was a very hard thing for him to do. He was not able to get to work in the winter, and now when he might have made some money by catching fish, he has no boat to go fishing in. Father has offered the 'Kingfisher' to John for the summer. The offer was made in such a way as can only be done by a thorough gentleman and a man of delicate feelings. My father respects the independence of the fishermen around here, and treats them as

*his equals, and they in return have a high regard and respect him.
John, although he hesitated at first to accept my father's kindness, finally agreed to do so if he could get no other work."*

CHAPTER TWELVE

Once a girl who we knew was bathing off the pier, at very low tide, with some others but none of us, and got into trouble which would, in all probability, have cost her her life when John appeared on the scene, sculling in from his boat. In less time that it takes to write the words he went to the rescue and pulled out the girl, for which she was gratefully presented $25.00 by my father.

John was a great friend of Bill. They used to spend hours together in this boat on the water, in fact he built the first "Kingfisher" I think. They talked little. One Christmas Bill sent him a box of candy, thinking you might like it, and ventured the next summer, to ask if it had been received, having heard nothing to that effect. The reply was that it had been, but what was immediately followed by a most emphatic: "Don't do it again!" Needless to say he never did.

In thinking of these days, it seems to me that one of my father's greatest pleasures was to watch the sunsets, of which we had a remarkably fine view, not only of the sky but of its reflection in the water. The great difficulty was that it generally came at the time of our supper, and as the dining room did not face the west, it meant leaving the table in the midst of the supper. This my father often did, for a longer or shorter time. Once I followed him to the end of the pier, where he was sitting, quietly enjoying the beauty, and as each little wave caught the color in its turn, he said with greatest feeling: "And God said, let there be light!"

One of my father's most cherished associations with Newport, went back to the days of the French Occupation, during the Revolution, when the Vicomte de Noailles was quartered on his great-grandfather, "Quaker Tom" Robinson, in the old house in Washington Street.

> You will find a full account of this in the bulletin of
> the Newport Historical Society, no. 42, which will
> not be given here

In August 1877, after an illness of two or three days our darling little Dempsey died in Newport. Edwin Crenshaw, father's old friend was visiting us at the time, which was rather hard for my mother, but he was considerate and kind as possible. We were all devoted to his little sister and her death was a great sorrow.

The next summer, 1878, we did not go to Newport, thinking an entire change would be better for my mother, accordingly we went, with grandmother, to a pleasant place in the country not far from Philadelphia, called fishing Creek, where there was a large settlement of Race Street Friends. Many of them were named Eve and came to yearly meeting in Philadelphia. It was wild and quite beautiful, but barely got settled when we discovered they were having an epidemic of typhoid fever, which Bill caught, greatly to the anxiety of our parents. Our stay was shortened, we children and grandmother leaving first to be followed by the others, when Bill was able to travel.

It was some time before he picked up from all his illnesses so has decided, next year, to send him to Phillips Andover Academy in Massachusetts, where the more bracing climate certainly helped him decidedly. He made a number of good friends there and much enjoyed the outdoor life, the walks in the country, the birds and flowers, and in the winter, the skating so much better than that around Philadelphia. Several of the boys came to visit us at Newport but the only one with whom we kept up a friendship was Robertson Trowbridge, in most ways about as different from Bill as possible, at that time he was quite delicate not at all outdoorsy, but much inclined to be a reader and student. He did not care for sailing, almost collapsed one day when Bill shot a gull from the boat, and the visit was not very thrilling for him or us, although the ladies threw themselves into the breach as much as they could. Robertson read aloud to my sister and me Howell's or Greens Short History of The English People, for which I was then struggling to my sister and me separately or together. With my mother he formed a most pleasant friendship, which lasted to the end of her life.

CHAPTER THIRTEEN

In recent years she wrote me a letter reminiscent of this first visit, saying how shy and strange he felt, never having seen people like us before. He said that soon after his arrival we went for a drive to show him some of the sights of Newport, my father driving, I never remember his doing, and on passing one of the new rather extraordinarily houses laughingly quoted:

He saw a cottage, with a double coach-house,

A cottage of gentility—

No one but Robertson knew what followed, and I can imagine how pleased my father was when he smiled and instantly "capped the verse" by saying:

And the devil did grin, for his darling sin Is pride that apes humility.

The Robinson House was full to overflowing in these days, for my mother made a point of asking our young friends and cousins, as well as several of my father's old cronies Tom and and Ned Rodman of Haverford days, Edmund Crenshaw and cousin Joe Coates, to visit us generally for a week or two. It was a strenuous life for my mother, but my father helped her at every turn, and they both thoroughly enjoyed it. My father always kept up to some extent, with the current cousins in Narragansett, and I well remember going with him to Peacedale and Wakefield, where our welome was sure to be a warm one. Soon after he began going to Newport regularly by father and cousin Saunders Coates the

Morton cousin of whom he was the most fond who spent his summers at Narragansett Pier, thought it would be a fine idea to locate the positions of their homes, by means of the rockets, some evening. Well do I remember the purchase and placing of the rockets on the porch, which at the time arranged, we set off simultaneously from both houses, a mark being made on the railing for reference. These years are strenuous for my mother but among the happiest of life.

My grandmother, her maid and the colored man who drove, for her for many years, and whose name, curiously enough, was William Rodman, were always part of the family. A horse was hired from a brother of John Barker, who lived near us on the Point named Bill Barker, who had a small livery stable and almost every morning and afternoon, the funny little old-fashioned carriage would appear on our door. Some one always had to go with our grandmother, whose favorite was the Avenue, curiously enough, with perhaps a very little of the Ocean drive, or of the country; we children often wondered what would happen if a fire alarm should come as in that case the horse always had to help pull the fire engine, but that contingency never occurred. In 1883 Daniel B. Smith died in is 91st year, and in 1888 Deborah Fisher Wharton's Horton's life was thus ended, in Newport, at 92 years. To the last everything that could be done for them, was done by their devoted children, and I can think of no people who better carried out both the letter and spirit of the great commandment; "Honor thy father and thy mother, that thy days may be long in the land that the Lord, thy God, giveth thee."

In 1889 my parents decided to take a short trip to Europe, which they never had been able to do before, and leaving Bill to join the party a little later, the rest of us sailed in April. Great was the interest of all the family and of our friends, when we, stay at homes started fourth on this venture. We had letters and cards, and gifts, and uncle Charlie branched out into Poetry (?) most unusual for him, only a short part of which is remembered.

To Ben.

Ben, dear Ben, good gracious Ben, When will this here business end? Kings, Queens, Emperors, Lords and Dukes, Will never pay for these here pukes!

A large part of the time was spent most delightfully in visiting the Cathedral towns of England. We took some pleasant little coaching trips in the country, Edward following on a bicycle, spent a few days with the Rev. J.T. Polock (whom Bill met quite by accident when he was looking up our Smith ancestor) at Brigham Vicarage, Carlisle, and my father worked on several family clues, with small success. He was most enthusiastic about everything connected with Scott, and I believe: "saw fair Melrose aright—visiting it by the Moon's pale light."

At Tintern(?) Abbey, to my horror, I saw him walking on a narrow wall high up and ivy covered with nothing to hold onto—but nothing happened except that his enthusiasm was heightened thereby!

We reached home safely, without any mishap, Bill started on law practice and we had much pleasure at talking over our experiences with our friends. Then came three supremely happy years to be followed on July 3. 1892 by Bill's death, at Newport when his boat, the "Falcon," capsized. It was on a Sunday morning that he, Ned Stewartson and Edward started in a smoky sou—wester, to sail around Rhode Island, from which only the latter came back to us. It was like a thunder bolt from a clear sky. He had already made for himself a place that was continually growing stronger in the community, in which he lived, his influence always being for the best things in life. My parents accepted this crushing blow in a way which was really inspiration to their friends a was a sure proof of the growth of their spiritual natures.

CHAPTER FOURTEEN

The following summer, 1893, the remaining members of the family, who had been drawn very close together, took a wonderful trip through the Canadian Rocky Mountains, then comparatively unknown. It was a great interest and beauty, and included a visit of two weeks at Sitka, in Alaska. We also stopped at the World's Fair in Chicago.

During the life of uncle Bob, he was the natural person to keep in touch with Grange and cousin Sam Morton, the last of the family to live there. After uncle Bob's death this fell to my father. For years his custom was to walk over once a week, and little Edward often went with him, the tie between them being very close. One day is my father was unable to go, I offered to take his place, that the boy might not be deprived of his walk; and was he disgusted! Finally he was unable to contain himself and burst out "Anna, thee goes entirely too fast, thee ought to stop and look at these things, which papa and I always do!; the things being the tiny plants growing in the cracks of the wall, on Shoemakers Lane, near the R.R. bridge.

My father came home from Newport once during the summer to see his father and cousin Susan Morton, when he slept at Grange in a special feather bed, and wasn't he delighted to get back to the sea breezes!

Another pleasant memory of these two good pals, is of the telling of the story, many times and oft repeated of how poor Mr. Brumer broke his ribs. He, at one time, gave my father lessons in German, which were needed for his work, and lived by himself out in the country somewhere, with steep flight of steps to climb.

One night he fell and broke his ribs, and in telling the story it was always necessary to feel pretty much all over the anatomy of the small boy, which involved a great deal of tickling and laughter.

My father was not the student and reader that his father was, but like his mother was familiar with best English classics, both prose and poetry, the favorite author of both being, I think, Sir Walter Scott. When we were children at school and had no studying to do in the evenings, my father quite often read to us, generally out of the Waverley Novels. He read the Scotch dialect very well and it was extremely pleasant until he came to a part which so affected his feelings, that he was obliged to stop, saying, with disgust: "confound it!" and beating a hasty retreat to the book room. He had a remarkable facility remembering quotation that were appropriate to little circumstances as they rose, and gave many a pleasant turn to the convsersation.

My father had the highest idea of personal integrity that I ever saw, and anything short of it was entirely unsatisfactory to him. He felt keenly the moral obligation of paying back the debts caused by the failure of the drug business, and never quite got out from under the cloud. For years, he set aside a tiny sum from a small income for that purpose, intending eventually to use the money from Grange. However, finally he became convinced that this was not in accord with his mother's will, which was that it should go to the use of his own family, so the plan was given up.

Rather soon after his retirement from business, my father became a Manager of the House of Refuge for boys and of which Daniel B. Smith was one of the incorporators. Among the active members of the board were Alfred and Frederick Collins, grandsons I think of second cousin of Deborah Morris Smith.

My father was a very regular attender of the Board Meetings and gave much of his time to the business they involved. He was the chairman of the Indenturing Committee for a number of years, and at one time was anxious to place some of the boys who had served their time at the institution on nearby farms, thinking it would be of mutual benefit. He got a list of the postmasters in the western counties of Pennsylvania each of whom was asked to send names and addresses of the farmers in his district, they, intern receiving circulars as to the project. We children thought it was fun helping but what was accomplished I do not remember. When the Board decided to adapt the Cottage System and move many of the boys to smaller buildings outside of the city my father contacted a man in Westerly, Rhode Island who had considerable experience in this kind of work. He moved to Philadelphia and the change was successfully made to Glen Mills.

CHAPTER FIFTEEN

One of the most pleasant memories I have of the things my father and I did together, is of a University Extension course of lectures in analytical botany, under Dr. J. T. Rothrock of the U. of P. It was in the evening and involved the short ride on the train, which did not faze us at all and I think the class enjoyed having an older person. We both passed the examination at the end. Father once told me he wished he had taken up a study of the compositae family when he was younger.

Of the three children that remained only two were married, Edward and I, which make two more stories for someone else to write later. You all remember my husband who is one of the last of the remarkable country practitioners, once so common, which interested my father very much, though thirty though they did not know each other at all well. Another Esther Morton was a great pleasure to Granddaddy, and he himself was revelation to Henry who never seen anyone like him.

Edwards choice of his life partner was a great satisfaction to my father, who was very glad that she would add another link in the chain that connected him with his favorite ancestor, Edward Wanton. How much he missed in not living to see their beautiful home life and their fine family, he, of course never knew.

My father's health was very good and as he grew older his physical powers only gradually became weaker, without any severe illness. He and my mother continued to walk arm in arm she always taking his arm, up and down the main street of Germantown, of which they were a well known and loved part, but the walks became shorter.

Several years before he died, he had a slight embolism of the brain, which left no great change in his condition, and he was happy and able to fill his delightful place in the family circle to the last. The evening of the night that he died a young friend of Esther's was at the house and when the time came for her to leave, my father, with his old-fashioned politeness, waited upon her to her home, very close by.

He went to bed and to sleep, and never wakened again in this world, Esther had a dog named "Skookum," and she told me that when our father's breathing became more heavy, showing that the damage was near, the dog, outside, began a mournful howling, which continued for some time, as if he knew in the passing of this soul, which he loved.

CHAPTER SIXTEEN

On March 31, 1904, my father's birthday, my mother wrote me a letter, which begins:

> *"This day thy father enters upon his eightieth year, and although he has aged much in the last decade, I still think that he scarcely bears the stamp of that age, and am sure no one more calmly and gracefully, more beautifully or benignly walked down life hill that he does.—"*

The two following extracts are also my mother's:

> *"No one ever seemed to me like him, but from him I feel that each of you (his children) has received some of his high and sterling qualities.—Not wishing to say too much or to scribe extravagant in any way, I who have lived with him for many years, can tell thee truly I never knew him to do a mean or ungentlemanly thing, while his whole conduct was based on goodness, truth and integrity—"*

> *"—It suddenly seemed as if I could hear thy grandmother Smith's voice work welcoming her dearly loved son, with some surprise too, "Why Ben has thee come.""*

Benjamin Raper Smith died on Easter Sunday, April 3, 1904, when the thoughts of great multitudes were filled with the Resurrection of the Spirit.

The following extracts are from letters written to my mother, at this time. From cousin Sally, the little bridesmaid at the wedding many years ago.

"My own precious aunt:

Without my saying a word, I am sure thee knows my heart tonight. My beloved uncle has been to me more than I can ever tell, and he will be still. I shall never feel him far away. Ever since I went as a little girl to sleep in the trundle bed, the tie between thee and me has been unbroken.

My precious uncle took me into his noble heart when thee married him, I always had a place there. A priceless privilege it has been to have been to me and mine. Oh Aunt Hetty dear, when thee can look back on all these years of cloudless love and mutual understanding and I always knew I had a place there. A priceless privilege it has been to have been tome and mine. Oh Aunt Hetty dear, when thee can look back on all these years of cloud-less love and mutual understanding I am sure that only gratitude and thanksgiving are in thy heart tonight even with thy great loneliness—."

From Anna Davis, oldest in her generation, who as a little girl used to pay visits to us in the summer in Newport with her brother Robert, where they made four generations under the same roof.

"My dear aunt Hetty

*I want to send just a word of love to thee and Esther
to let you know that we think of you a great deal, and
that we did love our dear Uncle Ben. He is associated
with some of the very happiest times of my childhood;
for the visits to Newport stand out clearly as perhaps the
greatest treats Robert and I ever had, and we can realize
now, as we could not then, how perfectly lovely each one
of you was in doing endless little (and big) services that
we might have a good time. Dear Uncle Ben's beautiful
courtesy and affection then, as always afterwards, made
an atmosphere which seemed to bring out the best in
everyone, and thee and he together I think we're perfect
as home-makers. Our younger generation honors your
lovely example and thee dear Aunt Hetty, we can feel
sure will go showing us how we all ought to accept what-
ever may come be sent us—."*

**The following was written and I think probably read by
Susan P. Wharton, another very intimate niece, at the funeral
services:**

*"To a good man of most dear memory this hour is sacred.
At peace with all the world, his noble spirit is at rest.
Pure strong child-like his tender heart and many little
acts of kindness and of love endeared him to us. And
what message has he left us? Forgive as ye hope to be for-
given. Blessed are the pure in heart for they shall see God
himself. Blessed are the merciful they shall obtain mercy.
And blessed are the peacemakers, the children of God.*

And then these other words to his companions: Blessed are they that mourn for they shall be comforted."

From Thomas R Rodman, of New Bedford.

"—-It seems almost an impertinence in the presence of greater and deeper sorrow to dwell upon my own, and yet it would not be right for me to with-hold my expression of the sense of what I have lost. Ours was an unbroken friendship for sixty-five years. It was variableness, it was never broken by one regret, the sharp incidents, rough angles that do so often mar the surface of a friendship. For he was not only pure, good and strong but he was gentle. I know of no one who more thoroughly realized the ideal of that grand old word, a Gentleman, and a true Gentleman. I felt so secure in his friendship.—-"

From cousin Kate Brickhead

"Anna Hunter has written me of dear cousin Ben's peaceful passing on, and with my heart full of the deepest sympathy for you all, I can but dwell on the blessedness of the end for him. It seemed so characteristic, so full of dignity, so gentle, so sparing of the feelings of others—I always had a very tender feeling for Cousin Ben, he was so uniformly courteous and sympathetic, two qualities that I care for especially and my dear mother felt the same, and I think she thought that he inherited them direct from his Mother (grandmother), that ideal great "aunt Morton" of hers—I have been through it all I

know that long years can never fill the gap and one can only comfort oneself with the thought of their peace.—"

From cousin Mary Willis.

"As I sat with you and your lovely home, last third day, my mind and thoughts were full of tender happy memories. From my earliest childhood Uncle Ben and thyself have been more than loving and kind to me. I told the children of Sally's and my visit to you upon your return from your wedding trip, and how we little girls enjoyed it, keeping thee company through the day and after tea going to bed and you two dear lovers, could be together. The dear nursery where we sat, was also full of memories of playing with those precious little girls, now both such fine women. I stood by the handsome peaceful body with thoughts of the many gracious welcomes everyone had received from him, and how much better we all are, for his beautiful influence.—"

From Henrietta C. Surtees a Wanton cousin living in England.

"His kindly friendship and pleasant cheering letters, will be a great loss to me, and we often spoke of him you all—recalling the pleasant incidents of our meeting. With his readiness for his call, how sweet it must be to you to know he was spared all suffering and entered into his rest in such a calm way—. Our cousin and kinship has been a pleasant one—"

From Mrs. Fairchild.

"In coming back here for the summer I am met by the most distressing news of your sad loss. 'We have lost Mr. Smith' is the way all the people speak: it is the whole Point who feel that it is a personal grief to miss the kind face, the wise voice, the upright mind, the tender heart—
—I can but feel how much your perfect companionship for so many years will be a stay to you now, when the past is so much fuller than the present—"

From William T. Richards.

"I was greatly shocked and grieved by the announcement of Benjamin's death—In a way I can measure your loss by my own for to me he was very dear. An ideal, a noble and lovely man. I know how changed and empty the world is to you and how helpless are words of sympathy. My heart aches with the knowledge of your sorrow, and I pray that your courage may be equal to the lonely days—" From Alfred Worcester.

"I am so glad of what must be the greatest comfort to you all,—that he not have the suffering of long illness and that he was at home. Such a home too! No one who has ever crossed that threshold—but has been surer of heaven for having done so. I am thankful I have the vivid memory of a recent visit. The good man then seemed so well: it was so lovely to see them returning from meeting together. I have always counted him among the very

few perfectly lovely souls I have ever known who lived on earth the life of heaven—-"

From Joseph G. Rosengarten

"(first name illegible) and Mrs. Dubois Miller and I are representatives of the House of Refuge, joined in paying last tribute and respect to your husband. His memory will be very precious to all of us, for services were char-acteristically conscientious, unselfish and useful. Apart however, from our association in that work, I look back through many years of friendship,—it was inherited from our fathers, for his father and mine were friends of long standing. Then too during our summers in New-port, your house was always very attractive, I can never forget the picture of Mrs. Deborah Wharton and Mr. Daniel B. Smith on either side of the of your fireplace. But Benjamin Smith had personal qualities of very highest kind that endeared him to all that knew him,—the Frenchman to whom in 1881 he showed to the Noailles gifts made to his ancestors a hundred years before, always spoke with respect and affection of his kindly interest in them,—and thus it was with all who had the good fortune to know him,—-"

From Brancel Lafarge, one of our young friends who was very dear to my father and returned his love. He wrote to Esther.

"I received your letter two days ago, it having been some-what delayed being a forward to me. (written when

family were in Paris). It is a pleasure to think you good father's passing away so quietly and happily near you all, as he had lived. I think I can realize what a loss it means to you and how you will miss him, yet as his death was so natural and at a time when he was full in years, you can at once treasure the memory of one whose life had given you so much. I am very, very glad to have you tell me that your father liked me, surely I was very fond of him and admired all this fine qualities which always made me feel when I was with him. It was an honor to know him, as it a delight now to remember him.—"

APPENDIX

OFFICE OF THE HOUSE OF REFUGE
1116 GIRARD STREET
PHILADEPHIA

Extract of Minutes

At a meeting of the Indenturing Committee of the House of Refuge, held at 1116

Girard Street, Wednesday, April 6th, 1904.

The Chairman announced the death of Benjamin R. Smith, for eighteen years

Chairman of this Committee, and presented the following Minute:

"The Indenturing Committee of the Board of Managers Of the House of Refuge, has heard with regret of the death of the late Chairman of this Committee; Benjamin R. Smith, and they desire to thus place on record their tribute to his long and faithful services in that position. The memory of his tireless and unceasing efforts in behalf of the Children in the care of this department of the work as well as in other directions; the hearty help and encouragement ever given to the Officers in charge of the indentured Boys and Girls; the universal courtesy shown to all connected with the Institu- tion, and his sterling integrity of Character; will ever be a bright page in the History of the House of Refuge.

On motion this minute was Unanimously adopted; and a copy ordered to be sent to his family. The Committee also request that this Minute be spread upon the minutes of the Board.

(signed) HENRY COPE

Chairman

Extract of Minutes

At a meeting of the Board of Managers of the House of Refuge,

Held Thursday, April 14^{th,} 1904, the following was unanimously adopted:

"Resolved that the Secretary be directed to record the following Minute, in recognition of the affection and esteem entertained for our late colleague, Benjamin R. Smith, who died April 3rd, 1904.

"Elected a member of the Board of the House of Refuge in January 1877, he was immediately elected a member of the Committee on Schools, and he became a member of the Inden- turing Committee in 1879, of the Committee on Buildings and Repairs in 1880, and the Committee on Cottages in 1894, all of which positions he held continuously until his retirement from active membership in 1896.

He was thus identified for nearly the whole period of his Membership in the Board with four of the most important of its committees, and in this way was at all times intimately. acquainted with the work of the House of Refuge of which he took his full share. His careful study of the problem of punishments and his elaborate report thereon, his personal and careful examination into the homes of the indentured children, and his intense interest in the home life of the boys at Glen Mills, which resulted in the creation of the Committee of Cottages, of which he was the first Chairman, are merely illustrations of unvarying sense of personal responsibility and willingness to assume any burden which might result therefrom.

His withdrawal to the retired list in 1896, brought to him A well earned respite from active duties, but was a distinct loss to his colleagues, and to the children committed to their care, and was the severance of most agreeable personal relations."

Resolved, that a copy of this minute be sent to his family by the Secretary.

Stamped with Seal of the House of Refuge
(and signed) RICHARD A. LEWIS

Secretary

DESCENDANTS OF BENJAMIN R. SMITH

Benjamin R. Smith, b. March 31, 1825, d. April 3, 1904: m. June 3, 1859; Esther Fisher Wharton, b. January 20, 18; d. March 4, 1915: daughter of William and Deborah Fisher Wharton.

Children

Robert Morton Smith, b. September 8, 1860; d. October 16, 1864. **William Wharton Smith** b, August 20, 1861: d, July 3, 1892, unmar. **Anna Wharton Smith**, b, January 24, 1864, m, June 3, 1898: **Henry Austin Wood**. M.D, b. October 9, 1855; d. February 22, 1942; son of Arbn Thayer and Ann Maria (Stearns) Wood.

Children

Ester Morton Wood, b. May 5, 1899; d. 1993 m. July, 1931 Gordon A. Bates, Son of Edward A. and Edith (Richardson) Bates.

Children

Anna Wharton Bates, b. August 18, 1933. d. 2010. **Mary Robinson Bates**, b. May 18. 1935. **Sarah Richardson Bates**, b. July 14, 1941

Elizabeth Hill Wood, b. December 12, 1900: m. September 14, 1932: Richard Burckes, b. March 27, 1894: son of John W. and Elizabeth (Berry) Burckes.

Children

Margaret Louise Burckes, b. August 3, 1935.

Children

Henry Austin Wood, Junior, b. December 31, 1903; m. May 28, 1928: Dagmar Lundholm,

b. April 25, 1903; daughter of Dr. Eric Mauritz and Anna (Olson-Sjoberg) Lundholm.

Children:

Henry Austin Wood 3rd, b. June 18, 1929. **Anna Wood**, b. August 8, 1930. **Benjamin Smith Wood,** b. May 19, 1905; m (1st) November 8, 1930: Annette Newhall Wright, b. July 14, 1903; daughter of William Redwood and Letitia Ellicott (Carpenter) Wright, m. (2nd), October 15, 1940: Barbara Rogers, daughter of Dr. Melville Forrest and Alice (Morse) Rogers.

Children

Benjamin Smith Wood, Junior, b March 30,1932; **Thomas Rodman Wood.** B. March 9, 1929 Letita Ellicott Wood, b. July 27, 1936. Ester Morton Smith b. April 3, 1865; d. March 18, 1942, unm. **Deborah Fisher Smith**, b. July 5, 1869; d. August 25, 1877. **Edward Wanton Smith**, b. January 18, 1875; d. August 27, 1940: m October 6, 1904:**Anna Dorothea Atwater**, b. June 27, 1877; daughter of Richard Mead and Abby Sophia (Greene) Atwater.

Children

Sarah Anne Greene Smith, b. May 29, 1906 d, January 20 1999, d. January 20, 1999. unm.

Ester Fisher Smith, b. August 11, 1908; m. September 15, John Howard Benson, son of Augustus Sherman and Elizabeth Perry (Howard Benson).

Children

Thomas Tew Benson, b. July 28, 1936, d, 1987; m. (1st) Elise Paumgarten (2) Anne Sherman.

Children

Oliver Hazard Benson

Samuel Roland Fisher Benson

John Everett Benson, b. October 8, 1939. M (1st) Ruth Fugiuele, (2nd) Karen Augeri.

Children

Christopher Ward Benson

Nicholas Waite Benson

Richard Mead Atwater Benson b. November 1943. d. June 22, 2017 m. Barbara Murray.

Children

Sarah Warren (Dave)

Luke Benson

Abby Benson

Daniel Benson

Anna Dorothea Smith, b. February 16, 1910; d. July 18 1939; m. August 23, 1930; m

August 25, 1930; Patrick Henry Hodgkin son of Henry Hodgkin. unm.

William Wharton Smith b. March 1, 1912 d. December 19 2005. m. April 30, 1943; (1st) Dorothy Gilpin Waring, Daughter of Bernard Gilpin and Mildred (Whitehall) Waring. (2nd) m. Claire Shoemaker,

Children

Marjorie Smith

William Smith 3rd

Daphne Stone

Robert Smith

Deborah Wharton Smith b. November 9, m. 1913; d September 24, 2002 m.(1st) May 23, 1941: Frank C. Lutman M.D. Son of Benjamin Franklin Lutman. b.

September 12: 1912. d September 1999, (2nd) Folsom Paul d. 24 2022,

Children

Richard Atwater Lutman b. November 6. 1943, unmar.

Christopher Greene Lutman d.2000 nc. b. 1946 d.2000

Sarah Anne Greene Smith b. August 23rd 1952.

Edward Lloyd Lutman b. August 25 1953 m. Thersa Elizabeth Kern.

Edward Wanton Smith; b.1920; d. March 2000; m. Patricia Ruth Woodward. d 2005.

Children

Joshua Woodward Smith. m. Kathy Seaburger

Children

Collin

Rodney Atwater Smith. m Tricia

Children

Sarah Anne Linden

www.ingramcontent.com/pod-product-compliance
Lightning Source LLC
Chambersburg PA
CBHW031455130726
47989CB00003B/1404